REFLECTIONS
FOR
LENT 2016

REFLECTIONS
FOR
LENT

10 February – 26 March 2016

STEVEN CROFT
ANDREW DAVISON
PAULA GOODER
MARTYN PERCY

with an introduction by SAMUEL WELLS

Church House Publishing
Church House
Great Smith Street
London SW1P 3AZ

ISBN 978 0 7151 4709 2

Published 2015 by Church House Publishing
Copyright © The Archbishops' Council 2015

The opinions expressed in this book are those of the
authors and do not necessarily reflect the official policy of
the General Synod or The Archbishops' Council of the
Church of England.

Liturgical editor: Peter Moger
Series editor: Hugh Hillyard-Parker
Designed and typeset by Hugh Hillyard-Parker
Copy edited by: Ros Connelly
Printed and bound by CPI Group (UK) Ltd, Croydon, CR0 4YY

What do you think of *Reflections for Daily Prayer*?

We'd love to hear from you – simply email us at

publishing@churchofengland.org

or write to us at

Church House Publishing, Church House,
Great Smith Street, London SW1P 3AZ.

Visit **www.dailyprayer.org.uk** for more
information on the *Reflections* series, ordering
and subscriptions.

Contents

About the authors

Stephen Cottrell is the Bishop of Chelmsford. Before this he was Bishop of Reading and has worked in parishes in London, Chichester, and Huddersfield and as Pastor of Peterborough Cathedral. He is a well-known writer and speaker on evangelism, spirituality and catechesis.

Steven Croft is the Bishop of Sheffield. He is the author of a number of books including *Jesus People: what next for the church?* and *The Advent Calendar,* a novel for children and adults, and a co-author of *Pilgrim: a course for the Christian journey.*

Andrew Davison is the Starbridge Lecturer in Theology and Natural Sciences at Cambridge University, Fellow in Theology at Corpus Christi College and Canon Philosopher of St Albans Abbey. He is the author of *Why Sacraments?, Blessing* and *The Love of Wisdom: An Introduction to Philosophy for Theologians.*

Paula Gooder is Theologian in Residence for the Bible Society. She is a writer and lecturer in biblical studies, author of a number of books including *Journey to the Empty Tomb, The Meaning is in the Waiting* and *Heaven,* and a co-author of the Pilgrim course. She is also a Reader in the Church of England.

Martyn Percy is the Dean of Christ Church, Oxford, one of the University of Oxford's largest colleges, as well as the Cathedral Church of the diocese of Oxford. From 2004 to 2014 he was Principal of Ripon College Cuddesdon. Prior to that he was Director of the Lincoln Theological Institute and has also been Chaplain and Director of Studies at Christ's College, Cambridge.

John Pritchard has recently retired as Bishop of Oxford. Prior to that he has been Bishop of Jarrow, Archdeacon of Canterbury and Warden of Cranmer Hall, Durham. His only ambition was to be a vicar, which he was in Taunton for eight happy years. He enjoys armchair sport, walking, reading, music, theatre and recovering.

Samuel Wells is Vicar of St Martin in the Fields, London, and Visiting Professor of Christian Ethics at King's College, London. He is the author of a number of acclaimed books; his most recent titles are *What Anglicans Believe, Crafting Prayers for Public Worship* and *Learning to Dream Again.* He was formerly Dean of the Chapel and Research Professor of Christian Ethics at Duke University, North Carolina.

About *Reflections for Lent*

Based on the *Common Worship Lectionary* readings for Morning Prayer, these daily reflections are designed to refresh and inspire times of personal prayer. The aim is to provide rich, contemporary and engaging insights into Scripture.

Each page lists the lectionary readings for the day, with the main psalms for that day highlighted in **bold**. The Collect of the day – either the *Common Worship* collect or the shorter additional collect – is also included.

For those using this book in conjunction with a service of Morning Prayer, the following conventions apply: a psalm printed in parentheses is omitted if it has been used as the opening canticle at that office; a psalm marked with an asterisk may be shortened if desired.

A short reflection is provided on either the Old or New Testament reading. Popular writers, experienced ministers, biblical scholars and theologians contribute to this series, all bringing their own emphases, enthusiasms and approaches to biblical interpretation to bear.

Regular users of Morning Prayer and *Time to Pray* (from *Common Worship: Daily Prayer*) and anyone who follows the lectionary for their regular Bible reading will benefit from the rich variety of traditions represented in these stimulating and accessible pieces.

The book also includes both a simple form of Common Worship: Morning Prayer (see pages 48–49) and a short form of Night Prayer, also known as Compline (see pages 52–55), particularly for the benefit of those readers who are new to the habit of the Daily Office or for any reader while travelling.

Making a habit of Lent

It's often said that life is about choices. But a life based on perpetual choice would be a nightmare. To avoid the tyranny of having to make perpetual choices, we develop habits. The point about habits is to develop good ones. That's what Lent is about. Here are the six most important ones.

- **Habit number one: look inside your heart.**
  Examine yourself. Find inside yourself some things that shouldn't be there. If they're hard to extract, get some help. Name them by sitting or kneeling down with a trusted friend or pastor, and just say, 'These things shouldn't be there. Please help me let God take them away.' Self-examination isn't just about finding things that shouldn't be there. It's also about finding things that are there but have been neglected. That's sometimes where vocation begins. Look inside your heart. Do it. Make a habit of it.

- **Habit number two: pray.**
  Don't get in a pickle about whether to pray with a book or just freestyle: do both. Once a day each. Simple as that. Think about the way you shop. Sometimes I shop with a list; sometimes not. Sometimes it's a pleasure; sometimes it's a necessity; sometimes it's a pain. Sometimes I go with someone else, or even help someone else to go; sometimes I go on my own. Sometimes it's about big things; sometimes it's about little things. Sometimes I really think carefully about it, and check through a kind of recipe list; sometimes I just do it, and realize later what I've forgotten. Prayer's just as varied. Just do it. Make a habit of it.

- **Habit number three: fast.**
  Fasting is about toughening yourself up so you don't go all pathetic at the first smell or sight of something sweet or tasty. It's about making yourself someone to be reckoned with and not a pushover. Make a pattern of life so you don't just drift to the mobile phone or email or internet as a transitional object. Stand in solidarity with those who don't get to choose. If you can't give up a single meal, do you really care about global hunger? And learn how to be really hungry. Hungry for righteousness. Hungry for justice and peace. Hungry, fundamentally, for Easter – hungry for the resurrection only God can bring in Christ. Do it. Make a habit of it.

- **Habit number four: give money away.**

'Ah,' you may say, 'I'm in a tight spot right now: I don't have any money.' Let me tell you now: there will never be a time in your life when you think it's a good time for giving money away. Try to tie your money to your prayers. Give money to something you believe in, and pray for the organisation you give money to. Just do it. Make a habit of it.

- **Habit number five: read the Bible.**

Imagine you were going into a crowded airport to meet someone you were longing to see but weren't sure you'd recognize. And imagine you had a photo album of pictures that showed them in a thousand different activities. Wouldn't you study that photo album so you'd almost committed it to memory? That's what the Bible is – a series of portrayals of God, and we study it to get to know God better so we'll have no recognition problems in a crowd. Genesis has 50 chapters: you can almost do it in Lent. You can get through a couple of Paul's letters a week. There's a dozen minor prophets: read a couple a week. Find a nether region in the Bible, and go digging. Buy an accessible commentary and follow a few verses each day. Just do it. Make a habit of it.

- **Habit number six: repair broken relationships.**

This is the last one and, for many people, the toughest. We've probably, many of us, got one big relationship that's all wrong – and maybe there's not a whole lot we can do about it. Maybe it's just a matter of keeping out of someone's way, if we've done them wrong, or trying to be civil, if they've hurt us. Now may not be the time to make things better. Now may not yet be God's time. But that doesn't mean we let all our other relationships get to that kind of place. Is there someone out there, a sibling, a rival, a long-time friend, a person who always felt inferior to you? Could you write that person a letter this Lent to say some things you've always appreciated about them but you've never told them? You can make it subtle. You can dress it up as something else. But could you see your way to that? And what about people whose names you don't know, people from whom you're estranged without ever having done the damage yourself? Could you make a new friend this Lent? Do it. Make a habit of it.

May you have a holy Lent, rooted and grounded in love.

Samuel Wells

The importance of daily prayer

Daily prayer is a way of sustaining that most special of all relationships. It helps if we want to pray, but it can be sufficient to want to want to pray, or even to want to want to want to pray! The direction of the heart is what matters, not its achievements. Gradually we are shaped and changed by the practice of daily prayer. Apprentices in prayer never graduate, but we become a little bit more the people God wants us to be.

Prayer isn't a technique; it's a relationship, and it starts in the most ordinary, instinctive reactions to everyday life:

- **Gratitude**: good things are always happening to us, however small.
- **Wonder**: we often see amazing things in nature and in people but pass them by.
- **Need**: we bump into scores of needs every day.
- **Sorrow**: we mess up.

Prayer is taking those instincts and stretching them out before God. The rules then are: start small, stay natural, be honest.

Here are four ways of putting some structure around daily prayer.

1 **The Quiet Time**. This is the classic way of reading a passage of the Bible, using Bible reading reflections like those in this book, and then praying naturally about the way the passage has struck you, taking to God the questions, resolutions, hopes, fears and other responses that have arisen within you.

2 **The Daily Office**. This is a structured way of reading Scripture and psalms, and praying for individuals, the world, the day ahead, etc. It keeps us anchored in the Lectionary, the basic reading of the Church, and so ensures that we engage with the breadth of Scripture, rather than just with our favourite passages. It also puts us in living touch with countless others around the world who are doing something similar. There is a simple form of Morning Prayer on pages 48–49 of this book, and a form of Night Prayer (Compline) on pages 52–55. Fuller forms can be found in *Common Worship: Daily Prayer*.

3 **Holy Reading**. Also known as *Lectio Divina*, this is a tried and trusted way of feeding and meditating on the Bible, described more fully on pages 6–7 of this book. In essence, here is how it is done:

- *Read:* Read the passage slowly until a phrase catches your attention.
- *Reflect:* Chew the phrase carefully, drawing the goodness out of it.
- *Respond:* Pray about the thoughts and feelings that have surfaced in you.
- *Rest:* You may want to rest in silence for a while.
- *Repeat:* Carry on with the passage ...

4 **Silence**. In our distracted culture some people are drawn more to silence than to words. This will involve *centring* (hunkering down), *focusing* on a short biblical phrase (e.g. 'Come, Holy Spirit'), *waiting* (repeating the phrase as necessary), and *ending* (perhaps with the Lord's Prayer). The length of time is irrelevant.

There are, of course, as many ways of praying as there are people to pray. There are no right or wrong ways to pray. 'Pray as you can, not as you can't', is wise advice. The most important thing is to make sure there is sufficient structure to keep prayer going when it's a struggle as well as when it's a joy. Prayer is too important to leave to chance.

+John Pritchard

Lectio Divina – a way of reading the Bible

Lectio Divina is a contemplative way of reading the Bible. It dates back to the early centuries of the Christian Church and was established as a monastic practice by Benedict in the sixth century. It is a way of praying the Scriptures that leads us deeper into God's word. We slow down. We read a short passage more than once. We chew it over slowly and carefully. We savour it. Scripture begins to speak to us in a new way. It speaks to us personally, and aids that union we have with God through Christ, who is himself the Living Word.

Make sure you are sitting comfortably. Breathe slowly and deeply. Ask God to speak to you through the passage that you are about to read.

This way of praying starts with our silence. We often make the mistake of thinking prayer is about what we say to God. It is actually the other way round. God wants to speak to us. He will do this through the Scriptures. So don't worry about what to say. Don't worry if nothing jumps out at you at first. God is patient. He will wait for the opportunity to get in. He will give you a word and lead you to understand its meaning for you today.

First reading: Listen

As you read the passage listen for a word or phrase that attracts you. Allow it to arise from the passage as if it is God's word for you today. Sit in silence repeating the word or phrase in your head.

Then say the word or phrase aloud.

Second reading: Ponder

As you read the passage again, ask how this word or phrase speaks to your life and why it has connected with you. Ponder it carefully. Don't worry if you get distracted – it may be part of your response to offer to God. Sit in silence and then frame a single sentence that begins to say aloud what this word or phrase says to you.

Third reading: Pray

As you read the passage for the last time, ask what Christ is calling from you. What is it that you need to do or consider or relinquish or take on as a result of what God is saying to you in this word or phrase? In the silence that follows the reading, pray for the grace of the Spirit to plant this word in your heart.

If you are in a group, talk for a few minutes and pray with each other.

If you are on your own, speak your prayer to God either aloud or in the silence of your heart.

If there is time, you may even want to read the passage a fourth time, and then end with the same silence before God with which you began.

+Stephen Cottrell

Wednesday 10 February

Ash Wednesday

Psalm **38**
Daniel 9.3-6, 17-19
1 Timothy 6.6-19

1 Timothy 6.6-19

'... godliness combined with contentment' (v.6)

At first glance this passage appears to be one of those classic killjoy passages: don't enjoy yourself, avoid money or any other form of enjoyment. Coming as it does on Ash Wednesday, it would be all too easy to read this as the command to misery for the next six weeks.

On closer reading, however, it is clear that in fact the message of this passage is quite the opposite. This is a passage that urges us towards contentment but reminds us of where this contentment can truly be found. The problem of money is that it is never enough. Those who want to be rich can so easily be sucked into wanting more and more, and hence into destructive and ruinous behaviours.

It is not money itself that is the problem but the love of money: a love that calls to us seductively telling us that this item or that activity will make us truly happy. It is interesting, in fact, that this passage does not use the word happy, nor indeed any word that can be translated 'happy'. Instead it uses two striking words: 'godliness' and 'contentment'. In other words, our aim should not be the immediate high of happiness but the worship of God, the one in whom we will find true life and deep contentment.

Almighty and everlasting God,
you hate nothing that you have made
and forgive the sins of all those who are penitent:
create and make in us new and contrite hearts
that we, worthily lamenting our sins
and acknowledging our wretchedness,
may receive from you, the God of all mercy,
perfect remission and forgiveness;
through Jesus Christ your Son our Lord,
who is alive and reigns with you,
in the unity of the Holy Spirit,
one God, now and for ever.

Thursday 11 February

Galatians 2.11-end
'... for fear of the circumcision faction' (v.12)

It is hard for us to appreciate the depth of feeling evoked by the debate about circumcision among the early Christians. Today, in our largely gentile Church, that Paul is right seems blatantly obvious, but to the early Christians this was very much not the case. At the time of Paul, *all* followers of Jesus were Jewish, as indeed was Jesus himself. It therefore seems obvious to them that everyone who followed Jesus would need to be Jewish. Paul's argument that they did not was bewildering and disorientating and had ramifications far beyond just 'ideas'.

One of the very practical ramifications of this was the whole question of who you could eat with. The problem was that if a Jew ate with gentiles, they became unclean and therefore could not go back to their normal life as a Jew without careful purification. It meant that Jews who followed Christ were cut off from their families and friendship groups. It is no wonder that Peter wobbled on this front – the implications of agreeing with Paul on the inclusion of gentiles went far beyond intellectual agreement. It was the emotional implications of his decision that seem to have caused Peter to come unstuck.

While we do not have exactly the same dilemma today, the issue of the emotional implications of our faith resonates in all sorts of ways and might make us feel a level of sympathy for Peter.

Holy God,
our lives are laid open before you:
rescue us from the chaos of sin
and through the death of your Son
bring us healing and make us whole
in Jesus Christ our Lord.

COLLECT

9

Friday 12 February

Galatians 3.1-14

'Who has bewitched you?' (v.1)

Paul's frustrations continue to boil away in this chapter. Here he is still talking about the issue of circumcision and whether gentiles need to be circumcised or not. Reading between the lines, what seems to have happened is that the gentiles who became Christians, while listening to the gospel that Paul proclaimed, have later been influenced by Jewish Christians who have persuaded them that it would be better to be circumcised. Paul's point here is that they had accepted the death of Jesus (v.1); they had already received the Spirit (v. 2) and they really did not need to do anything else in order to be a follower of Christ. Paul then goes on to use the example of Abraham whose faith established a true relationship with God without him following any of the Mosaic law; by extension the Galatians need do nothing more either.

Paul's frustration gets right to the heart of the Christian gospel. It is so easy to feel that there is always more to be done in order to be properly accepted as a Christian. It is not hard to imagine the Galatians almost sighing with relief in the knowledge that all they had to do was to be circumcised. The point is that they were wrong. They needed to do nothing more than accept God's gift and respond to him in faith. It really is that easy!

COLLECT

Almighty and everlasting God,
you hate nothing that you have made
and forgive the sins of all those who are penitent:
create and make in us new and contrite hearts
that we, worthily lamenting our sins
and acknowledging our wretchedness,
may receive from you, the God of all mercy,
perfect remission and forgiveness;
through Jesus Christ your Son our Lord,
who is alive and reigns with you,
in the unity of the Holy Spirit,
one God, now and for ever.

Galatians 3.15-22

'The promises were made' (v.16)

At this point in Galatians 3, Paul appears to be getting really rather convoluted. In order to make sense of what is going on, we need to recognize that Paul is using a very Jewish line of argument that pays close attention to the text and makes much of what he notices there.

His key argument is that God's fundamental covenant was with Abraham, a covenant that applied to him and to his 'offspring'. Paul understood 'offspring' to refer to a very particular offspring – Jesus. Therefore, while the Mosaic covenant was good, right and proper, it was superseded when Abraham's offspring – Jesus – arrived. His point, therefore, is that there is nothing, absolutely nothing, wrong with the law. It served its purpose and while it did, it was valuable. It just isn't needed now that Abraham's true offspring has arrived. Those who have faith in Jesus are incorporated into him and are automatically included in God's promise to Abraham.

This is one of those occasions where 'the workings' of Paul's argument are probably more confusing than the point he is trying to make, which is simply this: Abraham's faith was the foundation of his relationship with God; just like him we too can share in that relationship through our belief in Christ, and by doing so we inherit the promises of God's love and faithfulness first made to Abraham. Paul's argument may be complicated, but his point is simple.

Holy God,
our lives are laid open before you:
rescue us from the chaos of sin
and through the death of your Son
bring us healing and make us whole
in Jesus Christ our Lord.

COLLECT

11

Psalms 10, **11** *or* **44**
Genesis 41.25-45
Galatians 3.23 – 4.7

Galatians 3.23 – 4.7

'... all of you are one in Christ Jesus' (3.28)

There are some verses that we are so used to reading on their own that it can seem odd to come across them in a passage. Galatians 3.28 is surely one of those verses. It is so often quoted alone that we forget the context in which it is found in Galatians. Despite the fact that it is most often quoted in the context of the relationship between men and women, Galatians 3.28 is not primarily about that. As you will gather after reading the sweep of Galatians to this point, Paul is primarily talking about the relationship between Jews and gentiles; his examples of slave or free, male and female are additional examples but not more than that.

Paul's point here, then, is that it doesn't matter who we were before baptism; now that we are clothed in Christ, we are all one. He goes on in chapter 4 to talk some more about what this means – it means that we should act (and by implication treat others) as full heirs of God. We are able now to call God 'father' and so should treat each other as sisters and brothers of the one father.

The really important verses are probably not so much Galatians 3.28 as Galatians 4.6-7. Our ability to call God 'father' with all that entails is what transforms us, shaping our relationship with God and with each other.

Almighty God,
whose Son Jesus Christ fasted forty days in the wilderness,
and was tempted as we are, yet without sin:
give us grace to discipline ourselves in obedience to your Spirit;
and, as you know our weakness,
so may we know your power to save;
through Jesus Christ your Son our Lord,
who is alive and reigns with you,
in the unity of the Holy Spirit,
one God, now and for ever.

Psalm **44** *or* **48**, 52
Genesis 41.46 – 42.5
Galatians 4.8-20

Tuesday 16 February

Galatians 4.8-20

'I wish I ... could change my tone' (v.20)

If you are still in any quandary about Paul's seeming arrogance towards the Galatians, this passage may (or may not!) assuage your fears. After the full frontal assault of his opening chapter, Paul now allows us to see into his emotion and anxiety.

As we all know, a discussion by email can go badly wrong simply because we cannot see the facial expressions of the person writing to us and so can misunderstand what they are saying. It may be reassuring to know that this is nothing new. Lying behind what Paul says in this passage is his recognition that face-to-face meetings are much more effective than communication by letter.

It is important to notice that Paul's relationship with the Galatians began in vulnerability. We do not know what was wrong with him, but Paul was clearly ill when he first met them, and it was his illness that allowed him to proclaim the gospel (v.13). Letters like the one to the Galatians, opening in the way it did, make it hard for us to imagine Paul vulnerable, but he clearly was on many occasions (see also 2 Corinthians), and it was his vulnerability that seems to have made his ministry so effective.

Paul recognizes here that good relationships can only begin – and then be mended – face to face, because it is only then that we can see people for who they really are.

Heavenly Father,
your Son battled with the powers of darkness,
and grew closer to you in the desert:
help us to use these days to grow in wisdom and prayer
that we may witness to your saving love
in Jesus Christ our Lord.

COLLECT

13

Wednesday 17 February

Galatians 4.21 – 5.1

'For freedom Christ has set us free' (5.1)

In verse 4.21 Paul returns to his theme again. Back in his discussion about whether gentiles really need to embrace the entirety of the Jewish law and be circumcised, Paul now gives the example of a rather elaborate allegory. He reflects in an imaginative way on the Hagar and Sarah story. Although, to our modern eyes, Paul's argument appears odd, it would have made excellent sense to that part of his audience that was Jewish.

There are many examples from this period of Jews reading Old Testament passages as though they were a direct commentary on the world around them. This is what Paul is doing here, though we need to be aware of how offensive his likening of the Jews to Hagar was. They, of course, saw Isaac as their ancestor not Ishmael. This is why Paul uses this example; he challenges his audience to think deeply about ancestry, arguing that what makes you a descendant of Isaac is not so much bloodline as attitude – and, in particular, being truly free.

Christians are called to deep, abiding freedom, but our human nature sucks us back time and time again into slavery. Somehow we allow ourselves to be enslaved by others, by circumstances or by mental attitude. Christ has set us free, but staying free and refusing to be enslaved again takes an act of will.

COLLECT

Almighty God,
whose Son Jesus Christ fasted forty days in the wilderness,
and was tempted as we are, yet without sin:
give us grace to discipline ourselves in obedience to your Spirit;
and, as you know our weakness,
so may we know your power to save;
through Jesus Christ your Son our Lord,
who is alive and reigns with you,
in the unity of the Holy Spirit,
one God, now and for ever.

Psalms **42**, 43 *or* 56, **57** (63*)
Genesis 42.18-28
Galatians 5.2-15

Galatians 5.2-15

'... you were called to freedom' (v.13)

Real truth can often only be found in paradox. This part of Galatians serves up a great paradox, which requires profound reflection.

The Galatians are free. Christ has made them free. So they are now free to make any choice they want. The irony is that they have used their freedom to enslave themselves unnecessarily to the principles of some who argue that they 'must' do this, follow that and observe the other.

Real freedom, Paul maintains, can only be found in the choice to be slaves to one another, not because we should, but because we love. Love transforms everything, and if love is mutual, then there is nothing more freeing than acting as a slave out of love to someone who loves you. The vision of Christian community that Paul holds up here is a vision of a community whose members so love one another, so seek for the others' welfare, that it is the most freeing experience possible to be a slave within it.

The opposite vision that he introduces in verse 15 is spine-chilling – the vision of a community whose members so bite and devour one another with unloving demands and self-centred concern that it consumes itself. As Christians, we are not called to consume one another, instead we are called to the paradox that the greatest freedom can be found in choosing to act as slaves to one another in love.

Heavenly Father,
your Son battled with the powers of darkness,
and grew closer to you in the desert:
help us to use these days to grow in wisdom and prayer
that we may witness to your saving love
in Jesus Christ our Lord.

COLLECT

15

Lent

Galatians 5.16-end
'... the fruit of the Spirit' (v.22)

This passage follows on from the rest of what Paul has been saying for the whole of the letter, and it is worth remembering this as we reflect on a passage that is easier to get our heads around and therefore much better known.

Paul's image here is worth pausing on, not least because it is reminiscent of Jesus' teaching in places like Matthew 7.15-20, where he talks about trees bearing fruit that reveals what kind of tree they are. Paul's image is similar here. We need to be very clear that Paul is talking here of the fruit of the Spirit, not gifts of the Spirit. Gifts of the Spirit are optional: we all have some, but we don't all have them all. The fruit of the Spirit is not optional: we do not get to choose to have love and joy, for example, but not faithfulness and self-control (v.22).

Paul's point is that our life in the Spirit reveals who we are, but it also requires a positive choice to live in that way. A life lived in the Spirit will bear the fruit of the Spirit, but at the same time we need to choose to be guided by the Spirit; otherwise the fruit will fade and drop. The process works outside in as well as inside out. If we bite and consume one another as the Galatians were doing (5.15), then the fruit will fade pretty quickly.

COLLECT

Almighty God,
whose Son Jesus Christ fasted forty days in the wilderness,
and was tempted as we are, yet without sin:
give us grace to discipline ourselves in obedience to your Spirit;
and, as you know our weakness,
so may we know your power to save;
through Jesus Christ your Son our Lord,
who is alive and reigns with you,
in the unity of the Holy Spirit,
one God, now and for ever.

16

Psalms 59, **63** *or* **68**
Genesis 43.1-15
Galatians 6

Galatians 6

'... restore such a one in a spirit of gentleness' (v.1)

Paul's teaching is hard in two ways: sometimes it is hard to understand; at other times it is easy to understand but hard to do. Galatians 6 falls into the second category. In summary, Galatians 6 is about living in such a way that gives life and support for the good of all.

This chapter is a helpful corrective to the previous passage. It is easy to become so obsessed with our own spiritual life and well-being that we focus almost entirely on what fruits of the Spirit we have or do not have, and completely miss the welfare of those around us.

In this chapter, Paul points to the tightrope that we must walk in attempting to live a faithful Christian life. On the one hand, if we see people engaging in something that goes against the life of the Spirit, we should restore them with a spirit of gentleness (v.1). On the other hand, we need to keep a sharp eye on ourselves and ensure that what we are doing coheres with the life of the Spirit.

Paul's teaching is best summed up in verses 2 and 5: 'Bear one another's burdens' and 'all must carry their own loads'. Together these two give you the key to successful community living: compassionate care for those around us while at the same time taking responsibility for ourselves. If everyone in a community did that, it really would function for the good of all.

Heavenly Father,
your Son battled with the powers of darkness,
and grew closer to you in the desert:
help us to use these days to grow in wisdom and prayer
that we may witness to your saving love
in Jesus Christ our Lord.

COLLECT

Hebrews 1

'He is the reflection of God's glory and the exact imprint of God's very being' (v.3)

The opening of the Epistle to the Hebrews reads like a miniature creed, focused on the person of the Son. In four verses, it discusses revelation, the creation and preservation of the universe, the atonement and the ascension. At the heart lies a statement about both God and the incarnation. The Son, we read, is 'the reflection of God's glory and the exact imprint of God's very being' (v.3).

The Son redoubles the Father, as his exact reflection, and yet there is only one God, because that reflection is perfect. Only add the Holy Spirit, and we have the doctrine of the Trinity. With the incarnation, exactly the same principle applies: Jesus is the perfect image of the Father, made flesh. Jesus could therefore say of himself 'Whoever has seen me has seen the Father' (John 14.9).

If this seems rather abstract – although also important and true – then we might note that the word at the centre of these four verses has much to say about the Christian life. The Son is the 'exact imprint' of the Father. The Greek word is *charactēr*: the word for the stamp left in sealing wax. It is the origin of our English word 'character', meaning both our moral quality and the mark left by an inscription. The early Church linked these two meanings. Christians are to display the (moral) character of Christ and can do so because in baptism they are embossed with his life, as his brothers and sisters.

COLLECT

Almighty God,
you show to those who are in error the light of your truth,
that they may return to the way of righteousness:
grant to all those who are admitted
    into the fellowship of Christ's religion,
that they may reject those things
    that are contrary to their profession,
and follow all such things as are agreeable to the same;
through our Lord Jesus Christ,
who is alive and reigns with you,
in the unity of the Holy Spirit,
one God, now and for ever.

Psalm **50** *or* **73**
Genesis 44.1-17
Hebrews 2.1-9

Hebrews 2.1-9

'As it is, we do not yet see everything in subjection to them, but we do see Jesus' (vv.8-9)

This passage is very much addressed to the Church as it *now* exists, in between the triumph of Christ's resurrection and the final triumph of his return. It addresses a Church that has already been set on the right way, but which has not yet arrived, and which can therefore still wander. It addresses a Church that should, and does, contemplate the 'so great ... salvation' (v.3) that Christ has accomplished, but which still does not yet 'see everything in subjection to him': that is, with its proper order restored by being fully ordered to Christ. (The NRSV gives us 'in subjection to them', but the Greek is 'him'.)

Existing in this in-between state, the Christian receives at least three aids to a healthy perspective. The first is to acknowledge the real exaltation of Christ, and to be exultant in that: Christ *is* 'crowned with glory and honour' (v.9). The second is a due realism about what it means for the world still to be out of kilter, and especially to be out of kilter with Christ: for Christ it meant 'the suffering of death' (v.9), and for us, who are identified with him, it may also mean suffering. The third point picks up just that note of identification: whatever the Christian might go through, indeed whatever *anyone* might go through, we do so alongside Christ, who 'tasted death for everyone' (v.9). While Christ's death does not mean that no one else will die, it does change the character of death: we now have him alongside us, even there.

Almighty God,
by the prayer and discipline of Lent
may we enter into the mystery of Christ's sufferings,
and by following in his Way
come to share in his glory;
through Jesus Christ our Lord.

COLLECT

19

Wednesday 24 February

Hebrews 2.10-end

*'Since, therefore, the children share flesh and blood,
he himself likewise shared the same things' (v.14)*

Our reading today is full of the theme of sharing. Christ came to share sonship, for instance: the Son of God was incarnate in order to share with us what he has and is. He came so that he and we together might 'have one Father' (v.11). Sharing also runs in the other direction. Not only does God share what he is with us, but God also shares in what we are. Since those whom Christ came to redeem 'share' flesh and blood (it is what we have 'in common'), the Son shared this with us. Becoming flesh and blood, God now shares in what human beings share in common.

Theologians never tire of revisiting this dynamic of sharing, from God to us and from us to God. 'He became what we are, so that we might become what he is', wrote Athanasius (296–373 AD), among others. He took the *whole* of human nature upon himself, wrote Gregory Nazianzen (c.329–390 AD), since 'what he did not assume [or *share*], he did not heal'. Clement of Alexandria (150–215 AD) even went so far as to say that God created the human race 'for sharing' (*Paedagogus*, 'The Teacher', II.13). However, this emphasis on sharing at the centre of Christian thought, is not only, or necessarily, a comfortable idea; it also has ethical implications, as Clement recognized. If those who are wealthy should say 'I have more than I need, why not just enjoy it?' then, in Clement's estimation, they are neglecting sharing, and that is 'not properly human'.

COLLECT

Almighty God,
you show to those who are in error the light of your truth,
that they may return to the way of righteousness:
grant to all those who are admitted
    into the fellowship of Christ's religion,
that they may reject those things
    that are contrary to their profession,
and follow all such things as are agreeable to the same;
through our Lord Jesus Christ,
who is alive and reigns with you,
in the unity of the Holy Spirit,
one God, now and for ever.

Psalm **34** *or* **78.1-39***
Genesis 45.1-15
Hebrews 3.1-6

Thursday 25 February

Hebrews 3.1-6

'... the builder of a house has more honour than the house itself' (v.3)

God's work as creator is given forceful expression in an extended metaphor that runs through our passage today: 'the builder of all things is God' (v.4). This allows for a clear ascription of divinity to Jesus, since this 'builder' is identified as Christ: he is the one, as John put it, *through whom* all things were made (John 1.3).

God is the builder of all things. That lends a beauty to the trade or occupation that Jesus – we have every reason to suppose – learned from Joseph, his guardian. A boy of Christ's time would be all-but-expected to learn the trade of the man of the house.

Jesus, we read in the Greek, was a tekton (Mark 6.3). We typically translate that word as 'carpenter', but this may be too limited. It can mean a worker in any kind of material, a builder as much as to a carpenter. In the ancient world, the distinction between them was not so sharp. Joseph might put a coat peg in a wall, and Jesus after him, but he might also build the wall of the house. Certainly, Christ's parables suggest a familiarity with building towers (Luke 14.28-30) and with what sort of foundations withstand floods, and which do not (Matthew 7.24-7).

Reading Hebrews today, we can both rejoice in the dignity that the incarnate Son gives to workers of all sorts, not least to those who build, and rejoice in the poetry of the connection between Jesus the builder of Galilee and Jesus 'the builder of all things'.

Almighty God,
by the prayer and discipline of Lent
may we enter into the mystery of Christ's sufferings,
and by following in his Way
come to share in his glory;
through Jesus Christ our Lord.

COLLECT

Friday 26 February

Psalms 40, **41** *or* **55**
Genesis 45.16-end
Hebrews 3.7-end

Hebrews 3.7-end

'But exhort one another every day, as long as it is called "today"'
(v. 13)

The opening quotation today comes from Psalm 95. Known as the *Venite*, after its opening word in Latin ('Come, let us sing to the Lord'), it was once just about the most frequently recited psalm, since it was how morning prayer began every day, not least in the Book of Common Prayer but also in other rites with mediaeval roots. It still performs that task in the Roman Catholic morning 'Office of Readings'.

Today, in many Churches, we often like our Psalms sanitized. So, when Psalm 95 shows up, as it does reasonably often, although not as often as before, the final section is made optional. As if to serve us right, that excised section is all that the Letter to the Hebrews quotes.

These lines serve as a warning in the psalm and they serve as a warning in our Epistle: 'Take care, brothers and sisters', we read (v.12). But as always with the Gospel, the warning comes with an invitation, just as the invitation comes with a warning. 'Say yes to Christ', we are exhorted, and let those who have said yes not throw the gift of God idly away. Preserve urgency in the present moment, we are told, neither resting on our past laurels, nor deferring anything to the future. Remain before God in the present moment, and both the past and the future will look after themselves.

COLLECT

Almighty God,
you show to those who are in error the light of your truth,
that they may return to the way of righteousness:
grant to all those who are admitted
    into the fellowship of Christ's religion,
that they may reject those things
    that are contrary to their profession,
and follow all such things as are agreeable to the same;
through our Lord Jesus Christ,
who is alive and reigns with you,
in the unity of the Holy Spirit,
one God, now and for ever.

Saturday 27 February

Hebrews 4.1-13

'... while the promise of entering his rest is still open, let us take care that none of you should seem to have failed to reach it' (v.1)

Today's passage is about rest. In a striking conjunction of images, we are told that we should *strive* to *rest*: 'Let us therefore make every effort to enter that [eternal sabbath] rest' (v.11). In our time, more than ever, honouring rest in this way is often countercultural. Many of us have forgotten how to rest. If so, we can take God as our example. He may be, as we saw yesterday, the most active builder, but he is also the one who rests: 'God rested on the seventh day from all his works' (v.4).

The persistent metaphor for rest, running throughout the passage today, is of the sabbath: 'the seventh day'. For the Christian, the sabbath has become Sunday: not the seventh (and last) day of the week, but on what is called the eighth day – the first day of the new creation. If rest is countercultural, and if it is difficult for us to achieve, then the weekly Sunday sabbath presents an opportunity. On this day, more than any other, we are urged by the Church to look ahead and anticipate the world that is to come. Observing the day of the resurrection as a particular day of rejoicing and rest (as far as we are able) means at least three things: it is a countercultural witness; it is a way to discipline workaholic tendencies; and it is a foretaste of the world to come, of that 'sabbath rest [which] still remains for the people of God' (v.9).

Almighty God,
by the prayer and discipline of Lent
may we enter into the mystery of Christ's sufferings,
and by following in his Way
come to share in his glory;
through Jesus Christ our Lord.

COLLECT

Monday 29 February

Psalms **5**, 7 *or* **80**, 82
Genesis 47.1-27
Hebrews 4.14 – 5.10

Hebrews 4.14 – 5.10

*'Although he was a Son, he learned obedience through what
he suffered' (v.8)*

Two features of Israelite priesthood are mentioned in our passage:
every priest was *called* and every priest must *sympathize*. Those two
features are worked through, first in relation to the ancient Hebrew
priesthood and then in relation to Christ. The Hebrew priest had to
'deal gently' (5.2) with the wayward, remembering that he himself is a
sinner. The Greek here actually goes beyond externalities ('deal gently')
to the priest's inner life: he is to 'feel for' the people. As for the second
point, as we have seen, the priest is also *called*, since 'one does not
presume to take this honour' (5.4) – even if that calling comes through
family and birth.

What was said last about the ancient Hebrew priesthood is said first
about Christ. He was called, or 'appointed' by God. Then, just like the
priesthood of old, he is also full of sympathy. In his case, that follows
not from being a sinner among sinners, but from having suffered every
human woe as one of us. In a reference that reveals the author to be
familiar with Gospel stories, he invokes the agony in the Garden of
Gethsemane. Jesus, who was perfect as God, became also the perfect
human being. He was 'made perfect' (5.9), not in the sense of having
previously been lacking, but in the sense of having offered his life
perfectly to God, right to the end. In this way, his divinely perfect
humanity becomes what will perfect our errant humanity: 'having been
made perfect, he became the source of eternal salvation for all who
obey him' (5.9).

COLLECT

Almighty God,
whose most dear Son went not up to joy but first he suffered pain,
and entered not into glory before he was crucified:
mercifully grant that we, walking in the way of the cross,
may find it none other than the way of life and peace;
through Jesus Christ your Son our Lord,
who is alive and reigns with you,
in the unity of the Holy Spirit,
one God, now and for ever.

Hebrews 5.11 – 6.12

'... by this time you ought to be teachers' (5.12)

Yesterday we read about the perfection of Jesus. Today's passage is about the perfection of the Christian. The same Greek root underlies both the word for 'perfect' applied to Christ yesterday (5.9) and the word 'mature' today: 'solid food is for the mature' (5.14).

Progress in the Christian life is not always easy, and the part played by learning, thinking and the life of the mind was easily overlooked – it seems – in the first century, just as it is often overlooked now. Not that we are talking simply about abstract theological notions: the idea is of receiving a Christian understanding of the world; it is about habits of mind in those 'trained by practice' (5.14). In the Great Commission, Jesus told his followers to 'make disciples' (Matthew 28.19). We should not forget that the word means both 'one who has been disciplined or 'one who has learned'. The letter tells us to 'leave behind' various basic teachings (6.1). That is not because they are unimportant or forgettable. It is simply that, although irreplaceable, the foundation is not the whole building.

If the passage about the impossibility of repentance in certain circumstances is alarming, that is its main purpose. It warns the reader not to give up or to take the faith lightly, rather than being primarily a description of what might or might not happen to other people. Happily, the author of the epistle is 'confident' that his readers will not fall into these traps.

Eternal God,
give us insight
to discern your will for us,
to give up what harms us,
and to seek the perfection we are promised
in Jesus Christ our Lord.

COLLECT

25

Lent

Wednesday 2 March

Psalm **38** *or* **119.105-128**
Genesis 49.1-32
Hebrews 6.13-end

Hebrews 6.13-end

'When God made a promise to Abraham, because he had no one greater by whom to swear, he swore by himself' (v.13)

This is a passage about hope and why we have good grounds for hope. It is also a discussion of a knotty theological topic, namely whether God – who is free and sovereign – is under any obligations. We might say that 'God owes us nothing', and in a sense that is right. Whether that leaves you feeling a little uneasy depends on how you understand God. How do we know that God will not simply blot us out, or change his mind about loving us? Well, if God does not owe us anything 'absolutely' speaking, he does nonetheless owe it *to himself* to be true to himself. As the Anglican theologian Richard Hooker put it in the sixteenth century, in the opening of *The Laws of Ecclesiastical Polity*, 'the being of God is a kind of law to his working'.

That might satisfy the theologian, but God goes further. To make it all clear, God *promises* to bless us, as embodied in his promise to Abraham. What is more, God even swears 'by himself' since 'he had no one greater by whom to swear'. God binds himself to his own word by swearing upon himself, so that he would be bound to us and we to him. This is the ground for our hope; this is where the Christian can 'take refuge'; these are the grounds for hope, upon which we can 'seize' (v.18). This is what makes our hope both 'sure' and 'steadfast' (v.19), the first word meaning clearly and outwardly stable (like the outward oath) and the second meaning internally secure (like the character of God).

COLLECT

Almighty God,
whose most dear Son went not up to joy but first he suffered pain,
and entered not into glory before he was crucified:
mercifully grant that we, walking in the way of the cross,
may find it none other than the way of life and peace;
through Jesus Christ your Son our Lord,
who is alive and reigns with you,
in the unity of the Holy Spirit,
one God, now and for ever.

26

Psalms **56**, 57 *or* 90, **92**
Genesis 49.33 – end of 50
Hebrews 7.1-10

Thursday 3 March

Hebrews 7.1-10

'... resembling the Son of God, he remains a priest for ever' (v.3)

The author of Hebrews was fascinated by the figure of Melchizedek, for all he appears only twice in the Old Testament: first in the story of Abraham, as the priest of 'God Most High', who offers a sacrifice for Abraham after a victory in battle (Genesis 14), and then in Psalm 110.4, a messianic poem that likens the Davidic lineage to this mysterious figure. We will encounter that psalm verse tomorrow: 'You are a priest for ever according to the order of Melchizedek' (v.11).

Almost nothing is known about Melchizedek, and the author of our epistle makes something of this ignorance, in an almost playful mood. Look, he writes, Melchizedek appears in the Bible 'without father, without mother, without genealogy' (v.3) (making up that word for 'without lineage' as he goes). Melchizedek is like a figure from beyond time, turning up within the world, just like the Son of God, our author points out.

Yet, we might add, that is only half the story. The other figure in the passage is Abraham, and here that includes all of his progeny; Abraham acts on behalf of all of his descendents down the ages, present in his 'loins'. One of those descendants, we might point out, was Jesus. So, in the reading today we have both Melchizedek, symbol of the eternal and somewhat timeless priest, and Abraham, the symbol of human lineage. In Christ, both are embodied: the eternal and the time-bound, the mysterious and the earthy, a divine nature and a human nature.

Eternal God,
give us insight
to discern your will for us,
to give up what harms us,
and to seek the perfection we are promised
in Jesus Christ our Lord.

COLLECT

27

Hebrews 7.11-end

'... a better hope, through which we approach God' (v. 19)

We have encountered the idea of perfection in Hebrews before, but even for a letter that makes much of this concept, perfection is particularly prominent in today's passage (vv. 11, 19, 28, and 'for all time' in v. 25 could mean 'perfectly'). In the contemporary Church, we are most likely to encounter the quest for perfection as part of the heritage of Methodism and in the Roman Catholic Church. The quest for perfect holiness was an important part of the teaching of the Wesleys, and the Roman Catholic Church's veneration of the saints (with its parallels in Anglican churches) holds up examples of 'the spirits of the righteous made perfect' (Hebrews 12.23).

These traditions remind us of something important, that God's purpose is for us to attain perfection (v. 11). That is God's purpose just as much as it ever was (even if that was not ever attained before). The route to perfection, however, is radically changed compared to the old system of law and animal sacrifice. Something astonishing has happened with the birth, death and resurrection of Christ; something new has dawned ('arisen' in v. 15 has astronomical associations) – a priest has come from the tribe of Judah, rather than the tribe of Aaron, which is something archetypically unexpected for the letter's Hebrew readers. Through this unexpected priest, through this radical departure, the old goal of perfection is newly in view, and newly possible, maybe not in this life but certainly in the life to come.

COLLECT

Almighty God,
whose most dear Son went not up to joy but first he suffered pain,
and entered not into glory before he was crucified:
mercifully grant that we, walking in the way of the cross,
may find it none other than the way of life and peace;
through Jesus Christ your Son our Lord,
who is alive and reigns with you,
in the unity of the Holy Spirit,
one God, now and for ever.

Psalms **31** *or* 96, **97**, 100
Exodus 1.22 – 2.10
Hebrews 8

Saturday 5 March

Hebrews 8

'Now the main point in what we are saying is this ...' (v.1)

With chapter 8, we have arrived at the beginning of the extended, central passage of Hebrews, which deals with Christ as our high priest, interceding for us in heaven. It trades frequently on a contrast between the priesthood of the ascended Christ and the priesthood of the Old Testament, between the heavenly altar and the offering of Christ, and the human tent of temple and the sacrifice of animals.

The contrast certainly sets Christ in place as the new, perfect and eternal priest, but that but does not entirely demean the old priesthood in the process. The Old Testament priesthood had a value and a dignity, precisely because it was a likeness and foreshadowing of the eternal priesthood of Christ. It may have been only a 'sketch and shadow' (v.5), but that, again, is not to run something down, when the model is a 'pattern' based on the prayer of Jesus to his Father.

The Letter to the Hebrews is one of the most complicated books of the New Testament, so we can be grateful that the author provides us with a summary, here at the centre of the book, of what strikes him as its central message: we have a high priest, Jesus, who is right next to the Father, and who has the perfect offering to present, namely his own self – and what is more pleasing to God, who said of Jesus 'This is my Son, the Beloved, with whom I am well pleased' (Matthew 3.17)?

Eternal God,
give us insight
to discern your will for us,
to give up what harms us,
and to seek the perfection we are promised
in Jesus Christ our Lord.

COLLECT

29

Monday 7 March

Hebrews 9.1-14

'... through the greater and perfect tent' (v.11)

The Bible Museum in Amsterdam is well worth a visit. But if you are expecting to see lots of different kinds of bibles on display, you'll be disappointed. True, there are some important translations, including the first bible in Dutch. There is a garden of plants from Egypt and Palestine, and there are artifacts and archaeological objects from biblical times. But the centre-piece of the museum is the enormous scale model of the portable shrine erected by the Israelites after their exodus from Egypt and the model of the Temple Mount built in Jerusalem, a sacred place for the three religions: Judaism, Christianity and Islam.

What strikes many Christian visitors to the museum, looking at the models of the temple or Jewish shrines, is just how alien these constructions look today. Many synagogues can look quite like churches, but the Hebrew buildings for worship of the Old Testament were quite different. They had fire, animals, sacrifice, screened-off areas, inner sanctuaries, and some objects that were never to be looked upon by ordinary mortals.

The beginning of John's gospel (John 1.14) tells us that God became flesh and dwelt among us, but the more literal rendering of the verse is that God 'pitched his tent' among us. The writer of the book of Hebrews now claims that Jesus himself is 'the true tent that the Lord ... set up' (Hebrews 8.2). God, in Christ, has settled in the midst of the whole of humanity.

COLLECT

Merciful Lord,
absolve your people from their offences,
that through your bountiful goodness
we may all be delivered from the chains of those sins
which by our frailty we have committed;
grant this, heavenly Father,
for Jesus Christ's sake, our blessed Lord and Saviour,
who is alive and reigns with you,
in the unity of the Holy Spirit,
one God, now and for ever.

Psalms 54, **79** *or* 106* (*or* 103)
Exodus 2.23 – 3.20
Hebrews 9.15-end

Hebrews 9.15-end

*'... he has appeared once for all ... to remove sin
by the sacrifice of himself' (v. 26)*

There are several ideas and images that the New Testament presents to us that attempt to convey the meaning and the depth of Christ's death. Some of those ideas and images (such as 'ransom' or 'sacrifice') are imaginative metaphors that seek to communicate a range of complex truths. Our scriptures don't give us one single notion of atonement to subscribe to, but rather several that are simultaneously competitive and complementary.

The ones offered in today's scripture are essentially contractual. Even though images of blood and purity flow through the reading, the central issue is value. What is our value to God, and what is the value of Christ's sacrifice for us? The English phrase 'paid on the nail' relates to the bronze pillars, also called nails, that have large flat tops – the size of large plates or serving dishes. These nails can still be seen outside the Corn Exchange in Bristol and the Stock Exchanges in Limerick and Liverpool. From late medieval times, business deals were often sealed by money being exchanged on these large flat-headed nails. The songwriter and worship leader, Graham Kendrick's folk song from 1974 ('How Much Do You Think You Are Worth?') takes this idea up, and says that our lives have been valued, and 'a price had been paid on the nail' for each of us. The great beauty of the Christian story is that we can't get to heaven and abide with God in our own strength. The good news is that it is God who reaches down, touches us, bleeds and dies for us, enabling the door of heaven to be opened to all. Christ's death is a one-off, single payment for entry.

Merciful Lord,
you know our struggle to serve you:
when sin spoils our lives
and overshadows our hearts,
come to our aid
and turn us back to you again;
through Jesus Christ our Lord.

COLLECT

Lent

Wednesday 9 March

Psalms 63, **90** *or* 110, **111**, 112
Exodus 4.1-23
Hebrews 10.1-18

Hebrews 10.1-18

'... through the offering of the body of Jesus Christ once for all' (v.10)

One of the very best modern representations of the sacrifice and death of Jesus comes in a short story by Walter Wangerin, the Canadian writer. Wangerin's tale 'Ragman', features an old-fashioned rag-and-bone man, who tours the city and its slums. However, he does not look for valuable scrap or cast-offs. His cry throughout the city is that he will give 'new for old'. And the tale has a twist. He does not take objects, but rather the infirmities that cripple people, or render them marginalized and cast-outs from society. So, from a young girl with a bandaged head, dirty and stained with old blood, he takes the bandage and gives her a new bonnet, but the bandage he takes from her he now wears, and his blood flows freely through it.

In each encounter, the Ragman – a Christ-like figure – takes on the infirmities of all those he touches in exchange for their healing. He sacrifices himself for those he encounters. This idea would not have been strange to the early Church. 'For that which he [i.e. Christ] has not taken upon himself, he has not healed; but that which is united to his Godhead is also saved', wrote Irenaeus in his *Against Heresies* (c. 180 AD). Irenaeus understood that unless God had come among us in true humanity, and experienced our sense of desolation, suffering and despair, then these could not be redeemed.

Jesus redeems us through becoming one with us, for us, and of us. The word made flesh takes and transforms our frail bodies through his suffering and ultimate sacrifice.

COLLECT

Merciful Lord,
absolve your people from their offences,
that through your bountiful goodness
we may all be delivered from the chains of those sins
which by our frailty we have committed;
grant this, heavenly Father,
for Jesus Christ's sake, our blessed Lord and Saviour,
who is alive and reigns with you,
in the unity of the Holy Spirit,
one God, now and for ever.

52

Psalms 53, **86** or 113, **115**
Exodus 4.27 – 6.1
Hebrews 10.19-25

Hebrews 10.19-25

'Therefore, my friends, since we have confidence ...' (v.19)

How can we possibly have confidence? The word means 'to trust boldly'. Can we trust God in this way? The writer of the Hebrews is in no doubt. All we need to do is turn to God, and then realize that having turned, it will turn out fine if we are turned over to God. All we need to do is give back some of the love that has already been shown to us. Love is the lesson – the lesson that God teaches us, and asks us to practise with our fellow believers and the whole of humanity. We are to 'provoke' (!) one another to love and good deeds. As William Langland puts it in *Piers Plowman* (c. 1370):

'Counseilleth me, Kynde', quod I, 'what craft be best to lerne?'

'Lerne to love,' quod Kynde, 'and leef alle othere.'

So, the writer of Hebrews encourages us: we need not waver, but rather can hold fast to the one who holds fast to us. The God who has promised is faithful. There is nothing we can do that will make God love us any less or any more. God's love for us is full and complete, abundant and overwhelming. The mystics say that even God has one flaw – a frailty from which grace flows, which will teach us all we need to know about power made perfect in weakness. God's heart: it is too soft. And it is from God's open heart that we learn about God's open hands and embrace. So let us love one another, as God loves us.

Merciful Lord,
you know our struggle to serve you:
when sin spoils our lives
and overshadows our hearts,
come to our aid
and turn us back to you again;
through Jesus Christ our Lord.

COLLECT

Friday 11 March

Psalm **102** *or* **139**
Exodus 6.2-13
Hebrews 10.26-end

Hebrews 10.26-end
'For you need endurance ...' (v.36)

The Christian life is a marathon, not a sprint. Endurance is needed for the journey. Jesus, indeed, takes time to prepare his disciples with much advice on what to take for the road ahead. The rest of the New Testament testifies to the patience and endurance needed for the kingdom of God to be established. Like Rome, it won't be built in a day.

So we should not be surprised that passion and mercy meet in Jesus – because both are in the heart of God for humanity, and thus at the centre of our discipleship. The spiritual passion we are urged to embody is not just about the expulsion of energy.

The endurance we are asked to practise is not supposed to be about rationing our resources and energy: 'My soul takes no pleasure in anyone who shrinks back' (v. 38). So, we should not be allowed to blunt the energy and enthusiasm that flow from living the gospel. To be sure, orderliness and calculation have their place, but this should not be allowed to control and marginalize our passion for the gospel, because true religion, of course, is about extremes: extreme love, extreme sacrifice, and extreme selflessness that go beyond reason.

Religion in moderation is, arguably, a contradiction in terms. It should offend, cajole, probe and interrogate. One might say that a faith that does not get up your nose sometimes is hardly worth the candle. Endurance is crucial, but equally, don't hold back from proclaiming God's love.

COLLECT

Merciful Lord,
absolve your people from their offences,
that through your bountiful goodness
we may all be delivered from the chains of those sins
which by our frailty we have committed;
grant this, heavenly Father,
for Jesus Christ's sake, our blessed Lord and Saviour,
who is alive and reigns with you,
in the unity of the Holy Spirit,
one God, now and for ever.

Psalm **32** *or* 120, **121**, 122
Exodus 7.8-end
Hebrews 11.1-16

Hebrews 11.1-16

'If they had been thinking of the land that they had left behind ...'
(v.15)

As Søren Kierkegaard, the Danish theologian, said: 'Life can only be understood backwards; but it must be lived forwards.' In today's reading, we are given example after example of people who have lived forwards. They did not yearn for a return to where they had come from, but rather walked – by faith – into a new and uncertain future.

Often, this is the vocation of every Christian. But if this true, what are the next steps? How would you know you were called? How could you be sure? You can't of course, but there are two simple things to bear in mind.

First, have courage. Many journeys of faith and adventure with God never begin – because of fear. Fear of failure, or perhaps just of getting it wrong – suppose someone rumbles that I am just ordinary? Suppose I really make a mess of it? But failure is not the worst thing; letting it defeat you is. It takes a special kind of wisdom and courage to face failure and defeat, and then to try and move on from this.

Second, have patience. The Christian life is often lived more in waiting and hope than in results. Our journey of discipleship is weighed and measured over the entire course of a life. It takes a long time to appreciate just how much God has called us to. It takes daily devotion to see that our calling is not about affirmation or success at all, but rather faithfulness. Sometimes we are called not to win – even for God – but merely, by faith to walk with Christ.

Merciful Lord,
you know our struggle to serve you:
when sin spoils our lives
and overshadows our hearts,
come to our aid
and turn us back to you again;
through Jesus Christ our Lord.

COLLECT

Monday 14 March

Hebrews 11.17-31
'By faith Abraham ...' (v.17)

It's strange, isn't it, how our heroes of the faith also have feet of clay. Even in this impressive list – Abraham, Isaac, Jacob, Moses – the Bible does not spare us their fallibility and failure, as much as the Scriptures also applaud their faith. The key to this list is simple enough. God works through our strengths *and* weaknesses. This is part of what it means to try and cope with his grace. He can even use our imperfections for his glory.

This is clever stuff, to be sure. One of the artful things asked of us in discipleship is to check not only on what is going well – and what God is doing in that – but on what is not going so well – and what God might be doing in that too. This, indeed, is how God uses Abraham's foolishness. At the point where Abraham almost slays his son, God still speaks through this situation and fundamentally shifts Abraham's perceptions on worship and sacrifice.

This is why the Apostle Paul's well-known phrase is so vital to remember: 'power is made perfect in weakness' (2 Corinthians 12.9). God uses our weaknesses – even the foolish and base things of the world – to bring about change. He does not use Abraham, Isaac, Jacob and Moses because they are perfect. They are not. He uses them because they are willing, and will place their trust and future in God's hands. The list, then, is never quite complete. You can add your own name to this list too. By faith ...

COLLECT

Most merciful God,
who by the death and resurrection of your Son Jesus Christ
delivered and saved the world:
grant that by faith in him who suffered on the cross
we may triumph in the power of his victory;
through Jesus Christ your Son our Lord,
who is alive and reigns with you,
in the unity of the Holy Spirit,
one God, now and for ever.

Psalms **35**, 123 *or* **132**, 133
Exodus 8.20-end
Hebrews 11.32 – 12.2

Hebrews 11.32 – 12.2

'… let us run with perseverance the race that is set before us' (v.1)

Douglas Adams, in *The Hitchhiker's Guide to the Galaxy*, says that there is an art to flying. The knack lies in 'learning how to throw yourself at the ground and miss'. When we speak of falling, we can barely conceive of it in positive terms. To fall is dangerous … I have had a fall and broken a bone. We speak of fallen leaders, fallen men or women. The Fall ends the creation story in Genesis, and a fall begins the final chapters of our salvation story – Jesus falls on the Via Dolorosa.

The list of heroes of the faith today is a mixed bag. Some have succeeded outright, but others have failed – and conspicuously too. Yet God can even do great things with failure, because what matters to God is not success or failure, but faithfulness. The race that God asks us to run is like no other. It is more of a marathon than a sprint, and with few laurels at the end. Points don't mean prizes, alas.

Christians are called to follow a servant, not a winner – the one who led not by dominating, but by serving; the one who led not by triumphing, but by sacrificing; the one who led not by being first on the podium, but by falling to the ground and dying. It is from here we rise. For all discipleship requires us to give ourselves fully to God: to fall to and for him; to die with him, so that we might not only be raised, but also see the fruit grow from the many seeds that God is, even now, seeking to sow in his world.

Gracious Father,
you gave up your Son
out of love for the world:
lead us to ponder the mysteries of his passion,
that we may know eternal peace
through the shedding of our Saviour's blood,
Jesus Christ our Lord.

COLLECT

37

Wednesday 16 March

Psalms **55**, 124 *or* **119.153-end**
Exodus 9.1-12
Hebrews 12.3-13

Hebrews 12.3-13

'Now, discipline always seems painful rather than pleasant at the time ...' (v.11)

When Jesus speaks of himself as the true vine and of his father as the gardener (John 15.1) , he might have had in mind the same connections between discipline and discipleship that we find in today's reading. Jesus speaks of pruning (John 15.2), and Paul speaks of grace being poured out in Jesus (Titus 3.6). The bearing of fruit requires the gardener to be loving, encouraging – but also a pruner too. There is discipline in discipleship. Fruit takes time to grow.

Leslie Hunter (Bishop of Sheffield 1939–62), writing in *The Seed and the Fruit*, tells a parable about the world as it nears the end through war, famine and disaster. People, he tells us, begin to dream of a time when they can enter into a spacious store or shop in which the gifts of God to humanity are all kept. There is an angel behind the counter. The people cry out they have run out of the fruits of the Spirit and plead with the angel: 'Can you restock us?' The angel at first appears to refuse the request, prompting the people to complain bitterly that in place of war, afflictions, injustice, lying and lust, humanity now needs love, joy, peace, integrity, discipline – 'without these, we shall all be lost'. But the angel behind the counter can only reply: 'We do not stock fruits here ... only seeds'.

The reading today is about seeds growing fruit, the careful and disciplining husbandry that produces mature spirituality. There is no 'instant discipleship' – only one that is born out of a life of discipline, endurance and patience.

COLLECT

Most merciful God,
who by the death and resurrection of your Son Jesus Christ
delivered and saved the world:
grant that by faith in him who suffered on the cross
we may triumph in the power of his victory;
through Jesus Christ your Son our Lord,
who is alive and reigns with you,
in the unity of the Holy Spirit,
one God, now and for ever.

Psalms **40**, 125 *or* **143**, 146
Exodus 9.13-end
Hebrews 12.14-end

Hebrews 12.14-end

'... our God is a consuming fire' (v.29)

Christians, we are told, are to pursue peace with everyone, and attain a holiness without which no one can see God. It seems a tall order, especially when we are told that God is a consuming fire.

According to one Jewish tradition, we are all in the hands of God, but it is the souls of the righteous that 'will shine forth, and will run like sparks through the stubble' (Wisdom 3). So how shall we be? How shall we live? To answer this, you have to look into your heart and ask some searching questions. What random and costly acts of kindness and generosity will you perform today? Can you love and serve others – putting all before your self – and yet not count the cost? Can you, at the same time, radiate warmth, peace, openness and hospitality? Can you be a beam of God's light and warmth in a world that is sometimes dark and cold? Can your friends and colleagues say, hand on heart, that to know you is somehow to have been touched by the presence of God?

Christians, of course, know that they are not the fire; that is God. But Christians might know that they are the fuel for that fire. As one Eastern Orthodox prayer puts it: 'Set our hearts on fire with love for thee, O Christ, that in that flame we may love thee ... and our neighbours as ourselves.' Yes, our portion may be heaven, but we are here to glow, to light up the earth. May we, therefore, be a foretaste for others of the heaven prepared for us all.

Gracious Father,
you gave up your Son
out of love for the world:
lead us to ponder the mysteries of his passion,
that we may know eternal peace
through the shedding of our Saviour's blood,
Jesus Christ our Lord.

COLLECT

39

Friday 18 March

Psalms **22**, 126 *or* 142, **144**
Exodus 10
Hebrews 13.1-16

Hebrews 13.1-16

'Do not neglect to show hospitality to strangers ...' (v.2)

The theologian Mark Oakley says that 'Jesus is the body language of God'. The life Jesus leads expresses the wisdom of God. It is not just what he says; it is also what he doesn't say. It is not just what he does, but what doesn't do. His silence speaks as much as his words. His wisdom is embodied. And that is our calling: to let the Spirit of God dwell in us – to become a people where God is truly at home. The houses and homes that Jesus lived and stayed in tended to be pretty busy places – ones that practised God's hospitality. But with Jesus present, these were no longer ordinary homes. Many people came into these spaces and places for Jesus' teaching and healing ministry. The conversations and encounters that ensued were utterly transformative; both individuals and societies were changed. There is a sense in which our churches can also follow this – through gathering, convening and drawing all in, becoming an agent of God's gracious, proactive hospitality.

True Christian hospitality ought to make us a little uncomfortable; otherwise the dinner or lunch we offer is just like having friends over. The hospitality that Jesus exhorted his disciples to practise was one that broke down tribal barriers. It overcame divisions of race and gender, of age and class. Jesus welcomed all. That's why churches need to remember that it's not 'our altar' or 'our communion service'. It is Jesus' table; it is his meal. He desires to share with sinners. With the widow too, and the orphans, the prisoners, the lame, the leprous and the Samaritans. Jesus lives the hospitality of God. He now invites us to live and practise God's hospitable heart.

COLLECT

Most merciful God,
who by the death and resurrection of your Son Jesus Christ
delivered and saved the world:
grant that by faith in him who suffered on the cross
we may triumph in the power of his victory;
through Jesus Christ your Son our Lord,
who is alive and reigns with you,
in the unity of the Holy Spirit,
one God, now and for ever.

Saturday 19 March

Joseph of Nazareth

Matthew 13.54-end

'Is not this the carpenter's son?' (v.55)

It must have come as a shock to the friends, neighbours and family of Jesus. To discover that your son, cousin, brother or neighbour is gifted might not be such a surprise. The emerging revelation that Jesus is 'special' – and in what might be a unique way – would have caused many people to doubt their sense of discernment, and their intelligence. Their first reaction would be to try and contain and rationalize the perception. To admit otherwise would be to concede that, despite seeing plainly, they had in fact been blind all along. Few of us would rest easy with that sense of self-judgment.

So, what of this 'carpenter's son'? We know that by working in Joseph's trade – carpentry and building – he had, by living in Nazareth, been exposed to the nearby Roman town of Sepphoris, a Hellenized community of almost 30,000. So Nazareth, home to a mere 300, was a dormitory village supplying labour to a much larger cosmopolitan community nearby. It would have been full of gentiles of every kind.

This is significant. Jesus' kingdom of God project, from the outset, reached out beyond Judaism to the gentiles. Indeed, he often praised gentiles for their faith and often scolded the apparently 'orthodox' religion of his kith and kin for their insularity. Jesus saw that God was for everyone; he lived, practised and preached this. All this, arguably, made Jesus a great teacher for those beyond his neighbourhood, but not one that his own family and friends could easily take pride in. So the carpenter–prophet was honoured by many – but not in his own hometown.

COLLECT

God our Father,
who from the family of your servant David
raised up Joseph the carpenter
to be the guardian of your incarnate Son
and husband of the Blessed Virgin Mary:
give us grace to follow him
in faithful obedience to your commands;
through Jesus Christ your Son our Lord,
who is alive and reigns with you,
in the unity of the Holy Spirit,
one God, now and for ever.

41

Monday 21 March

Monday of Holy Week

Lamentations 1.1-12a

'Is it nothing to you, all you who pass by?' (v.12)

The first challenge of Holy Week is overcoming indifference. I'm not talking here about other people's indifference but our own. It is a hard thing to walk through the events the Church remembers in the next five days, even though we know that the cross leads to resurrection on Easter Day. It is a hard thing to follow the journey of the Lord we love through the pain and abandonment of his trial to his long and difficult death.

Reading Lamentations helps us prepare for that journey (and every other journey where we watch with compassion those who suffer). We are invited to lament, to attend to the suffering of the Holy City, personified, as she looks back on the day of her abandonment and chronicles her loss.

There are many emotions mingled together: regret, sorrow, repentance and shame. But the harshest pain (I think) is caused by the indifference of others to her suffering.

In the coming days there will be many distractions and many calls on our time. Is it possible to find time to sit and to be, and to overcome our indifference and our unwillingness to enter into this part of the story? As we enter into the suffering of Christ, so our hearts are softened in compassion towards others who suffer.

COLLECT

Almighty and everlasting God,
who in your tender love towards the human race
    sent your Son our Saviour Jesus Christ
to take upon him our flesh
and to suffer death upon the cross:
grant that we may follow the example of his patience and humility,
and also be made partakers of his resurrection;
through Jesus Christ your Son our Lord,
who is alive and reigns with you,
in the unity of the Holy Spirit,
one God, now and for ever.

Psalm 27
Lamentations 3.1-18
Luke 22.[24-38] 39-53

Tuesday of Holy Week

Lamentations 3.1-18

'He has made my teeth grind on gravel ...' (v.16)

These verses are a profound, anguished meditation on suffering. Once again the city 's pain is personified, its effects described in acute detail. All of this suffering is attributed to God, who is the subject of a series of verbs ('he besieged me ... he walled me about ... he shot into my vitals', vv.5,7,13).

These verses are agony to read and are still more painful to find yourself in when life is at its most difficult. However, I think the Lectionary makes a serious mistake in cutting off the reading at verse 18. Today we need to read on at least to verse 24 and possibly to verse 33.

Lamentations is not simply a raw cry of pain. Lamentations is poetry – a considered, albeit anguished, reflection on particular events in history. The poets have deliberately placed in counterpoint one of the starkest and most personal descriptions of pain and one of the most profound and rich affirmations of God's love.

Neither must be separated from the other in our reflection on the original context, nor in using these verses as a lens on Holy Week, nor in reflection on our own response to pain and suffering. The pain and difficulty in each may be more than we think we can bear. Yet there is a deeper truth still to be found in the midst of that valley.

True and humble king,
hailed by the crowd as Messiah:
grant us the faith to know you and love you,
that we may be found beside you
on the way of the cross,
which is the path of glory.

COLLECT

Wednesday 23 March

Wednesday of Holy Week

Psalm 102 [*or* 102.1-18]
Wisdom 1.16 – 2.1; 2.12–22
or Jeremiah 11.18-20
Luke 22.54-end

Jeremiah 11.18-20

'I was like a gentle lamb led to the slaughter ...' (v.19)

To the eye of faith, the Old Testament is full of images of the cross and kaleidoscopic patterns foreshadowing the life of Jesus. Some of these are in the great narrative of the story of Israel and of Jerusalem, as we have seen in Lamentations. Some are in the great institutions of Israel, such as the sacrificial system, as we will see tomorrow.

And some, as in today's reading, are in the lives of individuals. The reference here to the gentle lamb led to the slaughter is echoed in the great Servant Song of Isaiah 53 and again in John the Baptist's cry: 'Here is the Lamb of God who takes away the sin of the world!' (John 1.29). Although in Jeremiah 11 the image is one of innocent suffering, Isaiah 53 and John 1 go much further and connect the picture to the idea of a sacrifice offered on behalf of others.

However, the allusion to Jeremiah, the man of sorrows, takes us still deeper. Jeremiah more than any other prophet suffers for his message. Jeremiah more than any other prophet exposes his heart both to God in his prayers and to his readers in the oracles he leaves us. Seeing Jesus in his passion through the lens of Jeremiah gives new dimensions in our view of what is happening to the Man of Sorrows in this Holy Week.

COLLECT

Almighty and everlasting God,
who in your tender love towards the human race
    sent your Son our Saviour Jesus Christ
to take upon him our flesh
and to suffer death upon the cross:
grant that we may follow the example of his patience and humility,
and also be made partakers of his resurrection;
through Jesus Christ your Son our Lord,
who is alive and reigns with you,
in the unity of the Holy Spirit,
one God, now and for ever.

Psalms 42, 43
Leviticus 16.2-24
Luke 23.1-25

Leviticus 16.2-24

'Thus shall Aaron come into the holy place ...' (v.3)

Under the Old Covenant, the High Priest entered the Holy of Holies, the inner shrine of the tabernacle and the temple, on just one day of the year. The High Priest came into the holiest place only after the most elaborate ritual: an outer cleansing in water and dressing in special garments and then a spiritual cleansing through the sacrifice of a bull and, finally, the sending of the scapegoat into the wilderness, bearing the iniquities of the nation to a barren region.

On this day we celebrate the beginning of the New Covenant. On this day, in the course of the Last Supper, Christ gave meaning to the death he was about to suffer. In the words of Hebrews: 'he entered once for all into the Holy Place, not with the blood of goats and calves, but with his own blood, thus obtaining eternal redemption' (Hebrews 9.12). 'This is my blood which is shed for you...'

Christ made this offering so that you and I and all of humankind might ourselves come into the most holy place, the presence of the living God, cleansed and delivered from all sin and that we might enjoy friendship with God for ever.

Once again, the Old Testament image gives us both a foreshadowing of the greater salvation that is to come and a lens through which to view the cross of Christ: the inexhaustible well of our salvation.

COLLECT

True and humble king,
hailed by the crowd as Messiah:
grant us the faith to know you and love you,
that we may be found beside you
on the way of the cross,
which is the path of glory.

Friday 25 March

Good Friday

Psalm 69
Genesis 22.1-18
John 19.38-end *or* Hebrews 10.1-10

Genesis 22.1-18

'... but where is the lamb for a burnt-offering?' (v.7)

There is a peerless sentence in the Prayer Book service of Holy Communion: 'who made there (by his one oblation of himself once offered) a full, perfect and sufficient sacrifice, oblation and satisfaction for the sins of the whole world'.

The six central words are arranged in an ABCCBA pattern: sufficient sacrifice, perfect oblation, full satisfaction. However, it is the final part of the phrasing that always strikes me deeply when I say the prayer aloud: 'for the sins of the whole world'. The event we celebrate today must be a very great event indeed, larger than we can ever comprehend, however beautiful the language.

The story of Abraham and Isaac contains many resonances with the drama of Good Friday. The location (Mount Moriah, traditionally the temple mount); the father and the son; the wood that is first carried and then becomes an instrument of death; the love of the father for his son and yet a willingness to offer him, whatever the cost.

Yet, of course, there is a much greater drama before us today. For our Father in heaven does not hold back from the sacrifice of his Son. The Son goes willingly to his death out of love for his Father and for the world: a full, perfect and sufficient sacrifice, oblation and satisfaction for the sins of the whole world.

COLLECT

Almighty Father,
look with mercy on this your family
for which our Lord Jesus Christ was content to be betrayed
    and given up into the hands of sinners
    and to suffer death upon the cross;
who is alive and glorified with you and the Holy Spirit,
one God, now and for ever.

Saturday 26 March

Easter Eve

Hosea 6.1-6

'Come, let us return to the Lord' (v.1)

Repentance has many meanings. Here (as in the story of the prodigal son and the Emmaus Road), it means, quite literally 'to turn around'. The Hebrew word means 'to return'. We have been travelling in one direction, away from God, and now we deliberately change that direction and begin to come home. In other places, repentance is about renewal. The Greek word normally used in the New Testament means 'a change of mind and heart'.

In this sacred space between Good Friday and Easter Day, our goal should be repentance in both of these senses. As we contemplate the cross and the reality and cost of forgiveness offered to us, we set our minds and hearts to turn again back towards the Lord in all those areas where we have walked away or become indifferent.

As we look ahead to the cries of joy on Easter Day, to the reality of resurrection, we pray for our own renewal and transformation through the days of Easter, that we might become more like Christ, more ready to receive the Spirit.

Hosea reminds us that repentance in both kinds must be more than ritual, deeper than outward observance. What we offer to God must be the best fruit of our inner lives, longer lasting than the dew and the morning cloud: love that is steadfast, knowledge of God that is real.

Grant, Lord,
that we who are baptized into the death
of your Son our Saviour Jesus Christ
may continually put to death our evil desires
and be buried with him;
and that through the grave and gate of death
we may pass to our joyful resurrection;
through his merits,
who died and was buried and rose again for us,
your Son Jesus Christ our Lord.

COLLECT

Morning Prayer – a simple form

Preparation

O Lord, open our lips
and our mouth shall proclaim your praise.

A prayer of thanksgiving for Lent *(for Passiontide see p. 50)*

Blessed are you, Lord God of our salvation,
to you be glory and praise for ever.
In the darkness of our sin you have shone in our hearts
to give the light of the knowledge of the glory of God
in the face of Jesus Christ.
Open our eyes to acknowledge your presence,
that freed from the misery of sin and shame
we may grow into your likeness from glory to glory.
Blessed be God, Father, Son and Holy Spirit.
Blessed be God for ever.

Word of God

Psalmody *(the psalm or psalms listed for the day)*

Glory to the Father and to the Son
and to the Holy Spirit;
as it was in the beginning is now:
and shall be for ever. Amen.

Reading from Holy Scripture *(one or both of the passages set for the day)*

Reflection

The Benedictus (The Song of Zechariah) *(see opposite page)*

Prayers

Intercessions – a time of prayer for the day and its tasks, the world and its need, the church and her life.

The Collect for the Day

The Lord's Prayer *(see p. 51)*

Conclusion

A blessing or the Grace *(see p. 51)*, or a concluding response

Let us bless the Lord
Thanks be to God

Benedictus (The Song of Zechariah)

1   Blessed be the Lord the God of Israel, ♦
     who has come to his people and set them free.

2   He has raised up for us a mighty Saviour, ♦
     born of the house of his servant David.

3   Through his holy prophets God promised of old ♦
     to save us from our enemies,
        from the hands of all that hate us,

4   To show mercy to our ancestors, ♦
     and to remember his holy covenant.

5   This was the oath God swore to our father Abraham: ♦
     to set us free from the hands of our enemies,

6   Free to worship him without fear, ♦
     holy and righteous in his sight
        all the days of our life.

7   And you, child, shall be called the prophet of the Most High, ♦
     for you will go before the Lord to prepare his way,

8   To give his people knowledge of salvation ♦
     by the forgiveness of all their sins.

9   In the tender compassion of our God ♦
     the dawn from on high shall break upon us,

10   To shine on those who dwell in darkness
        and the shadow of death, ♦
     and to guide our feet into the way of peace.

Luke 1.68-79

**Glory to the Father and to the Son
and to the Holy Spirit;
as it was in the beginning is now:
and shall be for ever. Amen.**

Seasonal Prayers of Thanksgiving

Passiontide

Blessed are you, Lord God of our salvation,
to you be praise and glory for ever.
As a man of sorrows and acquainted with grief
your only Son was lifted up
that he might draw the whole world to himself.
May we walk this day in the way of the cross
and always be ready to share its weight,
declaring your love for all the world.
Blessed be God, Father, Son and Holy Spirit.
Blessed be God for ever.

At Any Time

Blessed are you, creator of all,
to you be praise and glory for ever.
As your dawn renews the face of the earth
bringing light and life to all creation,
may we rejoice in this day you have made;
as we wake refreshed from the depths of sleep,
open our eyes to behold your presence
and strengthen our hands to do your will,
that the world may rejoice and give you praise.
Blessed be God, Father, Son and Holy Spirit.
Blessed be God for ever.

after Lancelot Andrewes (1626)

The Lord's Prayer and The Grace

Our Father in heaven,
hallowed be your name,
your kingdom come,
your will be done,
on earth as in heaven.
Give us today our daily bread.
Forgive us our sins
as we forgive those who sin against us.
Lead us not into temptation
but deliver us from evil.
For the kingdom, the power,
and the glory are yours
now and for ever.
Amen.

(or)

Our Father, who art in heaven,
hallowed be thy name;
thy kingdom come;
thy will be done;
on earth as it is in heaven.
Give us this day our daily bread.
And forgive us our trespasses,
as we forgive those who trespass against us.
And lead us not into temptation;
but deliver us from evil.
For thine is the kingdom,
the power and the glory,
for ever and ever.
Amen.

The grace of our Lord Jesus Christ,
and the love of God,
and the fellowship of the Holy Spirit,
be with us all evermore.
Amen.

An Order for Night Prayer (Compline)

The Lord almighty grant us a quiet night and a perfect end.
Amen.

Our help is in the name of the Lord
who made heaven and earth.

A period of silence for reflection on the past day may follow.

The following or other suitable words of penitence may be used

Most merciful God,
we confess to you,
before the whole company of heaven and one another,
that we have sinned in thought, word and deed
and in what we have failed to do.
Forgive us our sins,
heal us by your Spirit
and raise us to new life in Christ. Amen.

O God, make speed to save us.
O Lord, make haste to help us.

Glory to the Father and to the Son
and to the Holy Spirit;
as it was in the beginning is now
and shall be for ever. Amen.
Alleluia.

The following or another suitable hymn may be sung

Before the ending of the day,
Creator of the world, we pray
That you, with steadfast love, would keep
Your watch around us while we sleep.

From evil dreams defend our sight,
From fears and terrors of the night;
Tread underfoot our deadly foe
That we no sinful thought may know.

O Father, that we ask be done
Through Jesus Christ, your only Son;
And Holy Spirit, by whose breath
Our souls are raised to life from death.

The Word of God

One or more of Psalms 4, 91 or 134 may be used.

Psalm 134

1   Come, bless the Lord, all you servants of the Lord, ◆
    you that by night stand in the house of the Lord.

2   Lift up your hands towards the sanctuary ◆
    and bless the Lord.

3   The Lord who made heaven and earth ◆
    give you blessing out of Zion.

**Glory to the Father and to the Son
and to the Holy Spirit;
as it was in the beginning is now
and shall be for ever. Amen.**

Scripture Reading

*One of the following short lessons or another suitable
passage is read*

You, O Lord, are in the midst of us and we are called by your
name; leave us not, O Lord our God.

Jeremiah 14.9

(or)

Be sober, be vigilant, because your adversary the devil is
prowling round like a roaring lion, seeking for someone
to devour. Resist him, strong in the faith.

1 Peter 5.8,9

(or)

The servants of the Lamb shall see the face of God, whose name
will be on their foreheads. There will be no more night: they will
not need the light of a lamp or the light of the sun, for God will
be their light, and they will reign for ever and ever.

Revelation 22.4,5

Into your hands, O Lord, I commend my spirit.
Into your hands, O Lord, I commend my spirit.
For you have redeemed me, Lord God of truth.
I commend my spirit.
Glory to the Father and to the Son
and to the Holy Spirit.
Into your hands, O Lord, I commend my spirit.

Or, in Easter

Into your hands, O Lord, I commend my spirit.
    Alleluia, alleluia.
Into your hands, O Lord, I commend my spirit.
    Alleluia, alleluia.
For you have redeemed me, Lord God of truth.
Alleluia, alleluia.
Glory to the Father and to the Son
and to the Holy Spirit.
Into your hands, O Lord, I commend my spirit.
    Alleluia, alleluia.

Keep me as the apple of your eye.
Hide me under the shadow of your wings.

Gospel Canticle

Nunc Dimittis (The Song of Simeon)

Save us, O Lord, while waking,
and guard us while sleeping,
that awake we may watch with Christ
and asleep may rest in peace.

1   Now, Lord, you let your servant go in peace:
      your word has been fulfilled.

2   My own eyes have seen the salvation
      which you have prepared in the sight of every people;

3   A light to reveal you to the nations
      and the glory of your people Israel.

Luke 2.29-32

54

Glory to the Father and to the Son
and to the Holy Spirit;
as it was in the beginning is now
and shall be for ever. Amen.

Save us, O Lord, while waking,
and guard us while sleeping,
that awake we may watch with Christ
and asleep may rest in peace.

Prayers

Intercessions and thanksgivings may be offered here.

The Collect

Visit this place, O Lord, we pray,
and drive far from it the snares of the enemy;
may your holy angels dwell with us and guard us in peace,
and may your blessing be always upon us;
through Jesus Christ our Lord.
Amen.

The Lord's Prayer (see p. 51) may be said.

The Conclusion

In peace we will lie down and sleep;
for you alone, Lord, make us dwell in safety.

Abide with us, Lord Jesus,
for the night is at hand and the day is now past.

As the night watch looks for the morning,
so do we look for you, O Christ.

[Come with the dawning of the day
and make yourself known in the breaking of the bread.]

The Lord bless us and watch over us;
the Lord make his face shine upon us and be gracious to us;
the Lord look kindly on us and give us peace.
Amen.

Love what you've read?

Why not consider using *Reflections for Daily Prayer* all year round? We also publish these meditations on Bible readings in an annual format, containing material for the entire Church year.

The volume for the 2016/17 church year will be published in May 2016 and features contributions from a host of distinguished writers: Jeff Astley, Joanna Collicutt, Jonathan Frost, Paula Gooder, Steven Croft, Helen-Ann Hartley, Libby Lane, Graham James, Helen Orchard, John Perumbalath, Sarah Rowland Jones, Tim Sledge, Angela Tilby and Margaret Whipp.

**Reflections for Daily Prayer:
Advent 2016 to the eve of Advent 2017**

ISBN 978 0 7151 4715 3
£16.99
Available May 2016

Can't wait for next year?

You can still pick up this year's edition of *Reflections*, direct from us (at **www.chpublishing.co.uk**) or from your local Christian bookshop.

**Reflections for Daily Prayer:
Advent 2015 to the eve of Advent 2016**

ISBN 978 0 7151 4457 2
£16.99 • Available Now

Reflections for Daily Prayer
App

Make Bible study and reflection a part of your routine wherever you go with the Reflections for Daily Prayer App for Apple and Android devices.

Download the app for free from the App Store (Apple devices) or Google Play (Android devices) and receive a week's worth of reflections free. Then purchase a monthly, three-monthly or annual subscription to receive up-to-date content.

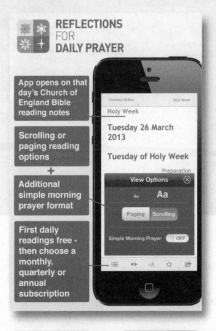

Reflections on the Psalms

Reflections on the Psalms provides original and insightful meditations on each of the Bible's 150 Psalms, from the same experienced team of writers that have made *Reflections for Daily Prayer* so successful.

Each reflection is accompanied by its corresponding Psalm refrain and prayer from the *Common Worship Psalter*, making this a valuable resource for personal or devotional use. Specially written introductions by Paula Gooder and Steven Croft explore the Psalms and the Bible and the Psalms in the life of the Church.

Also available
in Kindle and epub formats

£14.99 • 192 pages
ISBN 978 0 7151 4490 9

Reflections on the Psalms App

Reflections on the Psalms is also available as an app – both on Android and iOS. In the app version, each reflection is accompanied by the full text of the psalm from the *Common Worship Psalter*, plus a refrain and prayer.

The app allows you to follow a simple pattern of Psalms over the course of a month – following the 1662 Book of Common Prayer – or in any order you choose.

The app is available for a one-off cost of £8.99.

You can also watch this app in action on YouTube. Simply go to YouTube and search for 'Reflections on the Psalms app'.